The Light at the Edges

Deepti Kolte

INDIA • SINGAPORE • MALAYSIA

To my light, my constant.
My family

Table of Contents

1. Hello, How Are You? 9

2. Read Me 11

3. The Humble Coffee 13

4. Under the Gulmohar 17

5. Jupiter Through the Window 19

6. A Letter to the Rain 23

7. The Wait for the Rainbow 27

8. The Roses and the Lilies 31

9. Re: Me 33

10. The Full Moon 35

11. Golgappas 39

12. The Market 41

13. The Cherry in the Chaos 43

14. Paper Joys 45

15. A Fish in a Pond 47

16. The Lake 49

17. Your Sky 53

18. The Mime 55

19. Pretty Simple 57

20. The Bicycle Ride 61

21. Your Stroll, Your Run 65

22. Little Red Buds 67

23. Every Road Has a Story 69

24. Grass is Greener on the Other Side 73

25. The Thing About Lemons is... 75

26. Sparkles and the Rangoli 77

27. The Horizon is Where You Held My Hand 81

28. 6000 83

29. Just Words 85

Table of Contents

30. The Crossword 87

31. An Everyday Choice 91

32. The Camera 95

33. Before Tomorrow 97

34. Walk Alone if You Got to 99

35. The Child in You 103

36. Hold on Darling 107

37. Fallen but Not Broken 109

38. The Butterfly Hug 111

39. A Good Night's Sleep 113

40. Hope 117

Your Joys, Your Space *119-126*

The voids and the lows,
Some distant, some so close.
But they are open; the doors,
With a set of hopeful wedges.
Cross over these bridges,
For there is light at the edges.

A smile can hide a lot of pain.
Genuinely ask your dear ones how are they doing. Reach out.

Hello, How Are You?

I am fine, thank you.
Steady hectic work,
Busy weekend fun,
Movies, dinners,
Shopping and stuff,
All well, he smiles.
But how are you really?
I ask again to,
His tired eyes,
Unrested face,
Forced smile,
And frail self.
Not so well, he cries.
It's ok if you aren't fine.
It doesn't have to be always,
Fine, dine and shine.
Rest, you ought to.
Say no, if you have to.
Talk, you need to.
And cry, if you want to.

Books are a friend for life. When feeling lonely, when wanting to explore, when wanting to relax, when you just want to be, give them a chance.

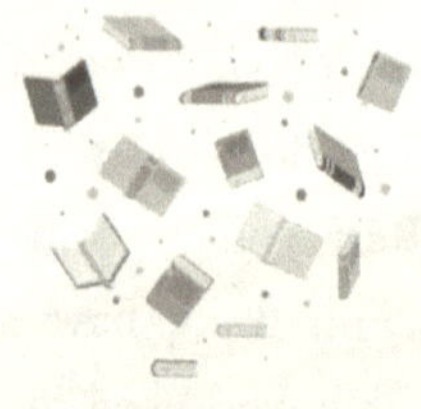

Read Me

Judge me by my cover or not,
There are words and words, a lot.

Spun into bed time stories,
Detailed into knowledge series,
Weaved into poems hearty,
Infused with inspiration quirky,
Inked into bios memorable,
Brushed into escapades unforgettable,
Treasures of ancient scriptures,
And louder than words, pictures.

Carry me in your bag,
Your purse, your desk, your swag.

Long annoying waits,
Tedium of travel spates,
Boring weekends,
Void of friends,
Sleepless confines,
Leisure times.

All have a fix in me,
To let you just be.

I won't let you down.
I will always stick around.
In your trusted small nook,
Read me, a wondrous book.

Love can happen over the humblest of things. Give it a chance.

The Humble Coffee

It was their first meeting,
Excited yet nervous,
Eager yet anxious,
One humbly early,
Other invariably late.

Holding at the only corner,
In a rather crowded spot,
In the humble coffee shop,
Stealing a coy glance,
With contagious smiles.

Un-decked out,
Dressed to dress,
Not impress,
Humble tees,
And casual gear.

Filter coffee shots,
Got them talking,
Vibing and sharing,
An idli vada,
And that humble bill.

Humble ramble,
Of work and likes,
Spirituality, hikes,
Cooking arbi and,
Planting trees.

And the after walk,
Star gazing, a little dance,
Leaving a chance,
For a definitely maybe,
And a humble coffee again.

**Change is inevitable, also difficult, but beautiful
and makes way for the new.**

Under the Gulmohar

I sat on a vacant bench,
Under the Gulmohar,
Without flowers,
Collecting a pale bunch,
Of the falling leaves,
Into my lap, as the breeze,
Softly and gently took them,
To the roots, into the sheaves.

We let go to go,
Where we came from,
And come back strong,
When it's time to grow,
Get our Gulmohar bustling,
With blooms and greens,
And turn a new leaf.
Sang the leaves rustling.

I carried the bunch, musing,
And spread them over,
As they traverse their,
Path of them becoming,
Into a new, bountiful,
While the beings await,
Through the transitions innate,
And see, change can be beautiful.

When you connect to something that feels greater than yourself, the result is pure joy.

Jupiter Through the Window

Tired sleepy eyes,
Woke up at its glimpse.
The moonlit night skies,
And a shining dot, that didn't blink.

I rejoiced.

As if a faraway friend,
Had come to say what's up,
In the mildly sweet night breeze,
Out of the window, I looked up.

The children of the universe,
Each in their grey, red, brown,
Are circling and probably happy,
In a world of their own.

Seemingly peaceful,
From a place of chaos.

Whilst the curious neighbours,
Admiring in awe & mesmerized,
Wanting to reach up,
Painted 'em into starry night.

Light years away.

Gases and rocks,
Volcanoes & storms,
Moulded into spheres,
Which shine back.

A speck for us,
A speck for them too.
And still,
Still, dark nights are beautiful too!

Sky was the limit for such,
Quantum of my thoughts.

As the moonlit sky got into slumber,
I slipped back into mine.
Stealing the tiny dot,
Into a blink divine.

Oh Jupiter!

When you let yourself fully immerse in the moment, you not only see but can also feel its tranquil beauty.

A Letter to the Rain

Dearest Rain!

Sad and sombre,
I sat by the window wing,
Watched you drizzle drops,
Like the beads in the string.

They made a song.
The rhythm started building,
As they trickled from the roofs,
Onto the grills and the railings.

I let you on my face,
Caressing it wet,
Washing away the worries,
Warming up the cold sweat.

Spread my arms and,
Caught you in my embrace,
For a moments rapture,
And a little dance of grace.

You do go wild at times,
And I wait for you to stop then.
But I also wait eagerly,
For your light mizzle again.

Marvelling at the scenes,
After you took a break,
Cleansed from the shower,
As if ruffled up and all awake.

I believe, we all have angels,
As I looked out at this new,
And I think you are mine.
You got me and I got you :).

26

**Rainbow colours our hopes, and its anticipation is our light at the edges.
Do you feel it too?**

The Wait for the Rainbow

A summer like afternoon,
Turned breezy mystic,
Said the walls in the room,
As they darkened in the moment.

Heavy sky was unburdening,
With the September showers,
And their light drizzle,
Blessing one and all unaware.

Window grills were pearled up,
And palms eager to hold,
Those little cute raindrops,
And sprinkle them all over.

But oh wait!

There was still a soft warmth,
Emanating through the dark clouds,
Making the other side,
Sunny, shimmery, boughed.

And suddenly the atmos was brimming,
With excitement and anticipation,
The drops and rays were preparing,
To draw up that arc of light.

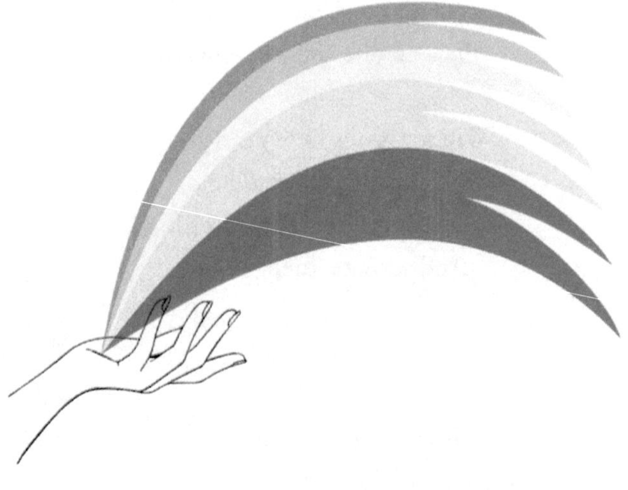

Looking up, missing a step,
Hopping on the wheel,
Scourging the whole sky,
For the artist's reveal.

And then there it was, with all seven,
Like a distant friend waving,
Bringing hope from the heavens,
For the unending hope.

Almost lacing an old building,
As the young, old, girls and boys,
All gathered and watched together.
(Such human desire to share the joys)..

Such an uplifting show!
I smiled absorbing,
The fading rainbow,
And the acoustics below.

Once in a while, take a pause, appreciate the wildflowers and the good that exists around you.

The Roses and the Lilies

The red loves the yellow,
And the yellow adores the red.
The roses and the lilies,
Tangled in a bouquet,
Were having a stifling day.

As they wondered, how these beings,
Won't take a moment of seeing,
To admire us and our pedigree,
In our pure, beautiful, uncut glory.
Wild flowers by the roadside,
Vibrant, fringing the park divide,
Rendezvous of flower valleys,
Pretty gardens in the alleys.

Follow the butterflies,
As airy, fluttering they visit you.
Pause and stop by the lilies,
The roses and orchids too.
There is pink, white, violet,
Flowers in such vibrant hues,
And also, a yellow and a red,
Bring back a handful with you.
Their fragrance to reminisce,
Wrapped up in a lovely calm,
Mellowing away all the stress.
…Now only if we could tell them,
Those busy beings; thought,
The roses and the lilies,
Wilting in a bouquet pot.

Take your chances. You have always got you.

Re: Me

I was sitting at the coffee table,
When it started to drizzle.
It's going to be a new start blithe.
The thoughts quivered like the,
Coffee vapours in the aisle,
Just as a marvelling me, a pluviophile,
At the rain glistening in the street light,
Worrying if I fail, who will guide me right?
I took a sip in the interludes,
Looking down at the small puddle,
Sometimes ripply and at times stagnant,
And I knew in those moments,
Just who would that be,
As I smiled to the marvel, i.e., me.

Even in the routine you can get your moon shot.

The Full Moon

Walking around running errands,
I look up and high,
To the dark quiet sky,
Eager, to catch your glimpse.
It's a lovely full moon night.
And the clouds can't cloud the sight,
And structures can't block,
And trees can't shadow,
You, in luminous aglow.
A fond look at you,
I smile and wonder,
It's as if all's in order.
Those stars around you,
Like buddies in blues.
The twinkle in my eyes,
Like the blink of your halo.
And even in the tedium, I got,
My very own moon shot.

The whiff of the rain-soaked soil,
Is beckoning you to take a break,
Eager to whisk away your sweat of toil.

Some sweet, some spicy, some sour; the blend of such moments is what gives life its flavours. Allow yourself to be open to savour them all.

Golgappas

It was a day,
When only Murphy's law worked.
Tired, sad, upset, irked.
Oh, such dismay!

A sombre me,
Sat on the stairs of a glitzy mall,
Watching people drift in the sprawl,
And that busy stall.

I got pulled.
The aroma and the tangs,
Power feeding my hunger pangs,
I drooled; it was my yang.

The golgappas!
The delightful savoury,
Few whole, few crumbly,
Got me satiated fully.

The day's got a flavour.
I mused watery-eyed at the twist.
Tangy, sweet, sour fix,
Like the Golgappa mix.

Enjoy and savour it,
It's all in the blend,
And all in your hands,
To taste it or leave it canned.

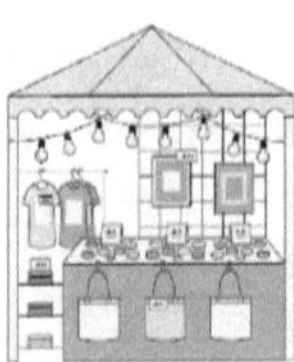

Markets give a glimpse of life. If you choose to look, every nook will be oozing with a different emotion and the farthest corners will have some hidden gems, waiting to be explored.

The Market

The market was calling,
For some mindless shopping,
Trinkets and flywheels,
Plethora of steal deals,
Big, small very small,
Shops had something for all,
Multi strings of lights,
Making the busy a shimmery sight,
Life less mannequins,
Staring into the din,
The buzz for the cotton candy,
The rabble near the sale standee,
Some penny level haggling,
And some carefree splurging,
The joy of getting a good bargain,
The disappointment at trying in vain,
Hands full with bags full,
Meandering to the colour pull,
Satin and garbs on display,
Choosing was no child's play,
One place and vibes a plenty,
Such that no one would go back empty.

Even when things don't go as per the plan there's always a cherry left. Look for it.

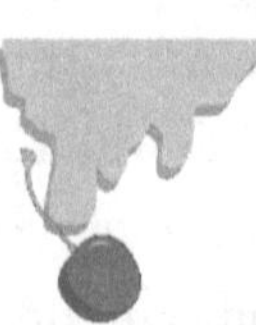

The Cherry in the Chaos

Plain vanilla,
Nutty delight,
Colour pops,
Sprinklers divine,
Dollops of scoops,
Full to the brim,
I sat with a cupful,
Of ice cream,
Watching,
The fun fair.
Cotton candies,
Balloon guns,
Merry rides,
Toy stalls,
Jumping jacks,
Can I have it all?
Excited eyes,
Taking a stroll,
With the cupful,
Like a butterfly on a prowl.
But oops!
The ice cream had melted.
Teary eyes,
Watched dejected,
Until they saw,
The red whole cherry,
And quickly gobbled it,
Very happy and merry.

Remember the joy of making paper planes out of rough papers? Such joys are precious, aren't they?

Paper Joys

A rough page from an old notebook,
Couple of folds and dart. Look!
Whose paper plane glides the smoothest,
And whose nosedives the farthest!

A rough page from an old notebook,
Couple of folds and swoosh. Look!
Whose paper boat floats the longest,
And whose sails the smoothest!

Doesn't matter who sails or glides,
None can sink the fun of thrilled eyes.
If not confined in the mind,
Simple joys aren't hard to find!

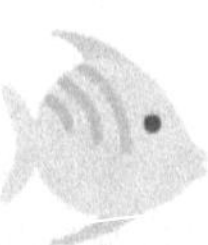

A little exploration can lead to discovering new connections.

A Fish in a Pond

A lone fish in a small pond,
A pond formed in the spring.
A golden yellow small one,
Swam in through a creek.
Lotus pond of whites,
Rocks and wood rose,
Bluebells and weed,
Resting, swimming, diving,
Into the depths, back to the brim.
Looking for a fellow fish,
When fins size of a petal,
Gently brushed past.
An ivory white small one,
Swam in from a distant creek,
And a small fish in a small pond,
Thanked the creek and the spring.

Nature in your neighbourhood is inviting you. Can you take out some time?

The Lake

Sunrises and sunsets,
Morning walks and evening runs,
Solo reveries and family outings,
Catch ups and practice meets.

Brown dragonflies unstuck,
A pretty pink lotus,
Green mosaic you can't un-notice,
And paddling flock of black ducks.

The skirting of trees,
Adorned in blossoms,
Of the colours of the season.
How my world allures!

I feel good when I get visitors,
Unfettering themselves,
From the tall rises,
Around the landlocked me.

Stepping in for a touch of fresh,
From the claustro streets,
The ruminating feet,
Looking for quiet trails.

Some actually see the quiet me,
Beyond the frame of their selfies,
As I reflect the magnanimity of the skies,
In colours of the day's hour.

Come see me,
Sit by the lakeside tranquil,
Pause, reflect, untangle,
Let us together feel good.

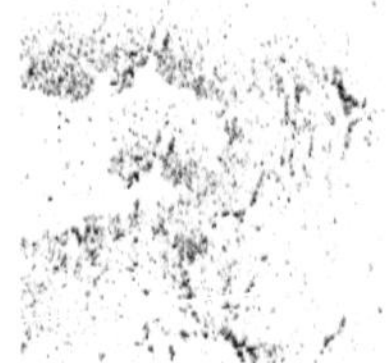

Be boundless and choose your sky, the sky beyond the self-imposed limits.

Your Sky

It's starry,
It's cloudy,
It's clear for few.

Shooting stars,
Faces in the clouds,
If you open your eyes to.

It's blue and pink,
It's black and orange,
If you look up at the hue.

It's your sky,
It's your limit,
If you decide so.

Change is the constant and can be so beautiful.
Nature shows us this in all its sublime forms.

The Mime

Puffs of clouds over,
Quiet afternoons,
Parched wind like a lover,
Journeying with the,
Yellowed leaves in a gather.

Into the grayscale vistas,
The wind rousing,
Fleetly from its siesta,
Rinsing the shadowed homes,
With a drizzling fiesta.

Fiery orange crown,
Atop the long tall trees,
The fall wind sliding 'em down,
Twigs, leaves and more leaves,
Adorning the earthy brown.

Somewhere deep blue,
And a chilly wind,
Somewhere hazy hue,
And a dormant world,
In a pristine cold view.

Such nature's mime,
Speaks beautiful change,
Seasons and fluid times,
Adapt, because constant,
Is the change, quaintly sublime.

**The pretty simple that exists around us has a
source of joy if we allow ourselves to acknowledge it.**

Pretty Simple

City life is not all easy,
Frantic and always busy,
I wondered why,
As I crossed over,
The skywalk, rather,
Bemusedly.

A sudden noisy din,
Of brakes and horns,
Jolted me back into the chaos,
(Well, from the chaos of the mind),
To deal with the nutsy grind,
As I kept finding my way (and a taxi).

Thank God for the company,
All through my journey,
A playlist of my favourite songs;
Got me through the jam,
While balleting like a charm,
I grooved in my mind.

The wait at the signal,
Was interrupted a little,
By tiny little hands,
Selling roses, pinwheels, tees,
And my heart muscled me,
Into buying their whole lot.

I reached home well.
Now hip hopping and hands full,
To the warmest hug,
A, how was your day,
And a hot tea tray,
Thinking all's well that ends well.

There's that pretty,
It's in the moments not just the city,
In such simple things,
In the everyday and the usual,
If we just let ourselves feel,
And see beyond the visible.

Tucked away in corners for later,
Smudged in hustles for the better,
Pushed under mounts of pressures,
It's all, right there for you,
Within you, around you,
That, pretty simple.

Fall and get up and try again. That's how your bicycle will go places.

The Bicycle Ride

She fell and oh so many times,
We both got bruised every time,
Lot of tears and bandaged tiny legs,
She got back on my big wreck,
Stumbling yet finding the balance,
Pedalling to go an extra distance,
Until the day she didn't fall.
And cycling we both had a ball,
Racing down the descends,
Piggy backing school friends,
Mindfully riding on exam days,
Speeding for the ice gola craze,
She knows; rather has learnt,
You fall but get up again stern,
And get on the bicycle, whereby,
You go places and get to fly.

Don't barter your warm cup of treats,
For the frosty unceasing schedules,
Make time to relish them hot and sweet.

Speed doesn't matter. What does is to keep moving, discover your own pace and what keeps you moving.

Your Stroll, Your Run

You see runners,
Focussed and gritty.
Warming up for a high five,
To the runners high.

You see strollers,
Absorbing the air.
Occasionally on a call,
All chill no rush at all.

You see brisk walkers,
They have a goal too.
Breeze past the strollers,
Aspiring to match the runners.

You see couplers,
It's their chance to catch up.
On the gossips, fam discussions,
The talks, with no interruptions.

You see joggers,
Comfortably reflecting.
Ear pods disconnecting them,
From the worldly humdrum.

Don't all walks seem fun?
Your stroll, your run.
Find your pace,
It's really not a race.

Can we escape the daily grind and the chaos around us? Not always. Can we be open to sudden small delights? Always.

Little Red Buds

The clock struck the usual,
Limping along the daily commute,
Harried faces on the wonted route,

Carrying and dragging the weight,
Of systems and the day ahead,
Street vendors, the din, such dread.

Concrete drilling piercing the air,
And listless aching souls,
Stumbling through the potholes.

Until cut in by a pretty sight,
Little many red buds beetling down,
On the soft green and earthy brown.

How something as beautiful,
Can flower in the midst of the disarray!
Exuding the wow in the day.

Limping along the daily commute,
The wonted route got such little treats,
Amid the clamour on the streets.

Open up, look beyond, seek out,
The beauty in everyday,
It makes everyday, feel less everyday.

Create your own path, the one that you really want to walk on.

Every Road Has a Story

I didn't know I could exist.
Through the wild wild bushes,
And their unmeasured spread,
There didn't seem a way ahead.

Tall trees of ages and their roots,
Marking the territory with their shoots.

But those exploring into the wild,
Bruising yet determined,
Made me steadily, with their zest,
A road into the forest.

I seemed impossible and daunting,
To those looking up in wonder.

But there were also those,
Who let their chisels,
Through the heat, wind & drizzles,
Grind endlessly until I emerged.
Taking them to the treetops,
On the mountain top.

I reform, I change, I adapt, I retreat.
The oceans fill me up as do,
The excited, pensive, tired and playful feet.
And I let all of them be.
In the tracks, deep in the sand.

Stranded beings.
Historic themes.
Potholes and honks.
Canopied walks.
Weekend moods.
Workweek blues.

Days same yet different flaunts.
I have been built to take,
The city, to wherever it wants.

**Comparison kills joy. Focussing on making your good
better will make your grass greener.**

Grass is Greener on the Other Side

The grass looks greener on the other side,
As he keeps watering it unsatisfied,
With his comparisons and glum cry.
While grass on his side withers dry,
As he keeps living in denial,
Of his rich greens and soil.

There can be more than one way of looking at any situation.
And sweet surprises await when you try to unravel.

The Thing About Lemons is...

The thing about lemons is,
They make the sour look wise.

The thing about lemons is,
It's a pinch of fresh with each squeeze.

The thing about lemons is,
A sugar cube takes away its fizz.

The thing about lemons is,
It's purple in yellow's guise.

The thing about lemons is,
It's a sour wiz.

Sour can be good.
Sour can be sweet good.
Sour can make bland good.
Sour can be just sour good.
Sour can be refreshing good.
And sour can be tickling good.

You have the power within. When you harness it,
the goodness is reaped by those around you as well.

Sparkles and the Rangoli

It's that time of the year,
The vibe's full of festive cheer.

There's hustle to get the brand new,
Gifts, sweets, greetings,
Sparkling decor and gatherings.

Week long preps,
The zest to get to every cobweb,
A lamp for every nook,
For that sparkling look.

The flowers,
The crackers,
The hopeful days,
The holidays,
And also, the Rangoli.

Pretty colours and the lines,
Dots and curves entwined,
Into a symmetric mosaic,
Powdered with sparkle thick.
Like a 'lil note for prosperity,
To enter in with gaiety.

The rangoli is for others to see too,
And the lamp is not contained within, oooh!

Their sparkles reach much beyond.

A moment of light, some colour pop,
Are enough to shine up,
The veiled pathways.
Dark corners needn't be dark always.

When you shine, you don't shine alone.

Your world basks in these sparkles,
of the smile you twinkled,
of the vibe you knit,
of the lamp you lit,
of the kind word you said,
of that distant call you made.

Be a sparkle for someone.

This is your cue to take a moment to express your love to your mother.

The Horizon is Where You Held My Hand

You held my hands at the dawn,
Tender curled, feathers of a swan.
With time they opened,
Knowing you will hold them,
When I dawdle like an open hem.

"Be a beginner every morn',
Create a path unborn,
Make your hard choices".
When I stumbled and looked up,
You had my hand and a tea cup.

When I faltered flat,
And heavy eyes looked at,
A worried, very worried you,
You smiled and held my hand,
Sending tears to a hinterland.

"Break the limits and explore,
Standing at the shore,
Won't fill the soul".
You were my steady anchor,
So, I could drift, learn, wander.

I walked, ran, paused,
Mushroomed and evolved,
For the horizon is where,
My mother held my hand,
Let me, be me and expand.

Not fighting our thoughts and accepting them can make a difference to how we feel.

6000

Thoughts six thousand a day,
The research says.
And how we thought,
We couldn't be busier!

But they are like travellers,
Short time revellers,
Each thought a chance,
To make a change.

Flow with them,
They'll drift.
Supress them,
You create a rift.
Accept them,
You'll love the shift.

Sometimes all it takes is a little encouragement, a sorry, a thank you, a hug to mend things.

Just Words

A plain paper turned purplish pink,
With the words written earnestly.
Through the shiny ink,
A thank you lit vividly.

The mind settled and unburdened,
When an envelope was delivered.
Wrapped in words unfeigned,
A sorry note was opened.

The face beamed with cheer,
When the words so rare,
Whispered into the ears,
You are enough dear.

The dimmed light flared up its rays,
With a pat on the back, long due,
And the words of praise,
I am so proud of you.

Tears went less deject,
And a smile swung in,
While the words wept,
As the hug did its thing.

A regular, chaotic or even a fun day has all the signals of a connected harmony. Just like a sequoia tree can lead to euphoria or the smell of old books can lead to that of the first rain in a crossword, there is such amazing connectedness in our lives as well.

The Crossword

Sequoia led to euphoria,
That led to exciting and aurora,
That led to vellichor and petrichor.

Crosswords are fun. Decipher and discover,
As one word opens up to another,
In such connected harmony.

As you go about doing your usual,
Look for such connectedness in the real,
And an affinity in your daily experiences.

Exhausted, you see a bench and sit to just be,
You relax and notice you are basking under a tree,
As you take a bite into your treat for all your work,
You gaze up only to be excited by the flock of birds,
But soon you head to the corner bookshop for shade,
And you soak up the charm of the sudden show of rains.

A crossword in your everydayness,
A harmony in the maze of wilderness,
Decipher and discover, the clues are out there.

Abbreviated spaces and gloomy soul?
Here's an amazing thing..
The light needs only a pinhole.

Why postpone what you can celebrate today?

An Everyday Choice

Birthdays arrive after a year,
Festivals too aren't always near,
New year, well, arrives in the end,
A handful parties cannot contend.

So, here's a thought.

Can everyday be a celebration?
Easy, effortless with no deliberation,
Making the bits count,
Precious and abound.

Let's see what have we got.

A barefoot walk on the grass,
Globe lights and smoothie glass,
A new unthought of hairdo,
A handwritten thank you,
Sing a song and a cuppa coffee,
Treat yourself, with an offhand toffee,
A pat on the back, rejoice for a while,
Each time you win big or small,
A surprise call to a distant close,
An impromptu plan to the improv shows.

Good food for thought?

You have this moment for sure,
Choose it over the unsure,
"It is a good choice",
Listen to your earnest inner voice.

While moments from the past make us nostalgic, living in the present moment is an opportunity to create more of such precious times.

The Camera

A mindless scrolling,
In the hours of nothingness,
Gets so very nostalgic,
As some pictures, like a witness,
To the times from the past,
Show up, to such happiness.

A picturesque yet lonely green mountain.
A portrait snap and a glow behind the lantern.
A cake smudged face and the wholesome laughter.
A woodscape stunning and the rapture thereafter.
A long shot of midweek karaoke of cacophony.
A two shot of tea lattes under the mahogany.
A finish line, a dainty medal and the runners high.
A fam gathering, vibes and just a smile shy.

These moments won't come back,
Precious memories from the past,
But living in the here and now is a life hack,
Until it becomes a memorable past,
And as such you keep building a lovely stack.

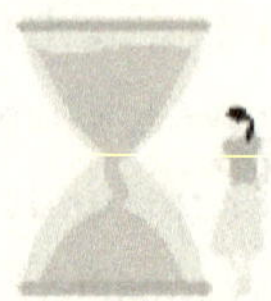

Don't let your dreams wait until tomorrow. Start today.

Before Tomorrow

Waiting for tomorrow,
Today got hopeful,
But tomorrow, said tomorrow.

So, sad today thought,
What if I stopped waiting,
For today is what I surely got.

So, a bit of resolve narrow,
To making a start,
Put today before tomorrow.

There is more than one way to reach your place. And with experiences for your company, there is no feeling alone.

Walk Alone if You Got to

I started walking alone,
Alone and inert wasn't an option,
Options to discover near and far,
'How far' could I go.

And as I did, I found paths,
Paths so different reaching the same place,
A place, a destination, a corner,
A corner busy with little things.

A tea stall under a tall tree,
A tree bursting with trumpets of blossoms,
Blossoms that had left a soft trail,
The trail that led me there.

The hot tea and its rustic flavour,
Flavour that opened up the capped mind,
Mind toggling from stuck to unstuck,
Unstuck to keep walking.

And I left again to keep walking,
Walking for the same place on a different trail,
A trail to the known through the unknown,
Unknown showed me 'how far'.

I noticed some are rough with stones,
Stones carpeted with flowers and the lonely,
The lonely blurring to a smooth tar busy,
Busy hustle on nothing but just the tar,

Fellow lone walkers on their ways,
Ways separate some, and crossing few,
Few pause, smile and move on,
Moving on to keep walking, alone or not.

The only way to reach your place.

As we grow, over time we get disengaged from
what use to bring us pure happiness.

The Child in You

There was once a child.

To be happy was no big deal,
Play, smile and just squeal,
A candy pop, a crayon stick,
Enough to do the happy trick.

Then the child grew up.

Life got tough & not so kind,
Stress, reason & all that chime,
To be happy was a big deal,
Candy won't trick the zeal.

It was a fine day.

When driving through the mundane,
Tiny hands knocked on the window pane,
It was a child selling tiny knick-knacks,
Buy or not, he was all play with his tiny pack.

He watched and adored.

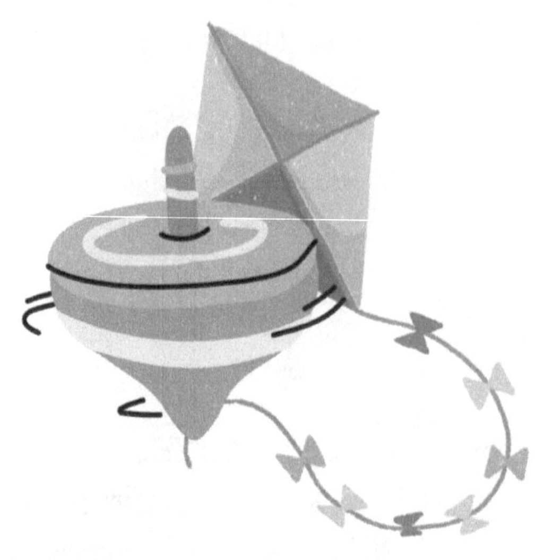

They were a happy lot,
Happy, just like that,
But there was a bout of unease.
Someone he knew was amiss...

Where was that child?

Who could smile for no reason,
Who knew simple was fun,
Who would see a puddle,
And jump right in the muddle.

Be silly at times.

Who would hear a song,
And dance all along.
The child in him, was missing,
Lost and forgotten while growing.

He would bring him back.

The little joys and so much fun,
A swing, a prank, a crayon,
Some lollipops, marbles and clay,
Life can always have some child's play.

Hope is out there. Try to look for it and hold on.

Hold on Darling

When all you can is despair,
The day is a strenuous affair,
Only thing you want, is to do nothing,
The weight of regrets is crushing,
When you don't think all will be well,
To fight it, you smile a tad too well.
Hold on darling.
There is always hope, look for it,
You are always enough, know it,
Change happens and that doesn't change,
And it's ok to not feel ok or strange,
As much as it saddens,
Take each day as it happens,
For the sun doesn't go away.
And the clouds won't stay.

When you choose hope, you rise, no matter how deep you fall.

Fallen but Not Broken

I stood the mighty me.
They relaxed in my shade.
And over gossips and tea,
New bonds were made.

While some beings built,
A nest, and some a swing,
Some scratched me with no guilt,
Hearts and their arrows piercing.

Some painted me on a canvas new,
Few figments of their imagination,
And my branches looking up to the blue,
With rave admiration.

Those were such green days.
But now I stand axed and reduced,
Making way for the concrete daze,
But holding my ground, resiliently fused.

What I have are some branches,
Weathering such seasons,
And a soft rustle in the bunches,
When the wind circles with no reason.

I have fallen but not broken.
Some still paint me on the canvas new,
Only figments of their imagination,
....and the blue.

**Be there for yourself. Be kind to yourself.
Give yourself that butterfly hug.**

The Butterfly Hug

It's about to give in and implode.

Everything's falling, breaking within.
Ploughing through the debris of fears around,
The clogged voice and the moist eyes.

Don't know how to speak up.
The impending anxiety is just muffling.
Don't know what will happen next.

Can the moment just freeze?

This too shall pass.
A deep breath, open arms,
And a kind smile.

The clogged voice and the moist eyes,
Found a release,
In the butterfly hug.

Embrace your emotions. Don't shut them. Don't shun them. Anger is yours. Sadness is yours. Grief too. As joy too.

A Good Night's Sleep

Behind the rose-coloured specs,
The world appears rosy.
But the eyes behind them,
Know also the thorns so rosy.

A hard day, a harsh word,
Pressures and regrets,
Rejections and long nights,
Sleepless they start to get.

Is it anger you feel or hurt?
Are you impatient or annoyed?
Are you sad or lonely?
Unappreciated, filling up a void?

Sweet wins and gifts,
Meeting with pals,
Heard your fav song?
Or climbed a mountain tall?

Is it joy you feel?
Are you proud or content?
Are you elated or hopeful?
Just thankful or exuberant?

A change, a loss,
A rainy day, a lonely dinner,
A test, a decision,
A breakup and spilled water.

Is it grief you feel?
Are you afraid or stressed?
Are you anxious or worried?
Feeling low or depressed?

All emotions are yours,
To be embraced and not shut,
To be felt for what they are,
To be recognized and not shunned.

For that's when you know,
What to heal, and what to keep.
And that's how you get,
A good night's sleep.

Hope pushes us to keep going. And that's how miracles unfold.

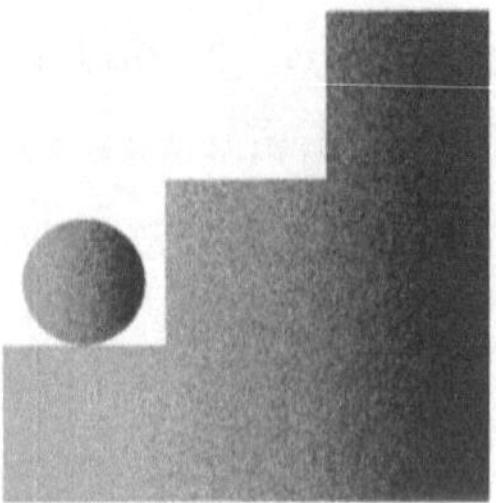

Hope

Hope is a good thing,
They all say,
So, I thought let's try.

I started my days hopeful,
All very bright,
Expecting miraculous strides.

Didn't see miracles though,
But some hope,
I kept pushing up on the slope.

Because keeping up, is uphill,
But with hope nudging,
Onwards started happening.

On every plunge and despair,
Hope was a cue,
And attempts at the new, grew.

Small wins added up to a miracle,
Hope, the word,
On each tiny step forward.

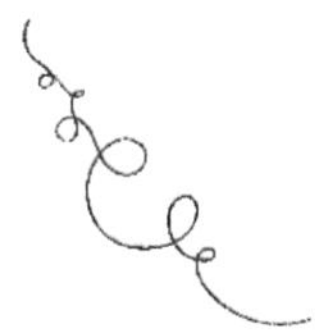

Your Joys,
Your Space

Your space to write out the small things that bring joy to you.

____

____

____

____

____

____

____

____

Your space to write out the small things that bring joy to you.

**Your space to write out the things that made you smile
when you least expected it.**

____

____

____

____

____

____

____

____

**Your space to write out the things that made
you smile when you least expected it.**

**Your space to write about the people that made a
difference to you in any way.**

**Your space to write about the people that made a
difference to you in any way.**

____

____

____

____

____

____

____

____

Don't go looking for the sunshine.
See your face light up,
When your smile breaks out of the confines.